Telling the Bees

Ann Kelley

with
illustrations by
Mark Foreman

Oversteps Books

First published in 2012 by   Oversteps Books Ltd
                                6 Halwell House
                                South Pool
                                Nr Kingsbridge
                                Devon
                                TQ7 2RX
                                UK

www.overstepsbooks.com

Copyright © 2012 Ann Kelley
ISBN 978-1-906856-27-4

All rights reserved. No part of this book may be reproduced, stored in a retrieval system, or transmitted in any form, or by any means, electronic, mechanical, photocopying, recording or otherwise, or translated into any language, without prior written permission from Oversteps Books, except by a reviewer who may quote brief passages in a review.

The right of Ann Kelley to be identified as the author of this work has been asserted by her in accordance with the Copyright, Designs and Patents Act 1988.

Printed in Great Britain by imprint digital, Devon.

Supported by the National Lottery through the Arts Council England

To Michael Bayley for invaluable advice and patience over the years.

And to true friends Jenny Strong and Jan Relf, and writer friends Marion Whybrow, Juliet Trewellard, Chris Higgins and Liz Kessler, for listening.

And grateful thanks to Mark Foreman for his illustrations.

Acknowledgements:

Some of these poems have been published by:
London Magazine, Rialto, Agenda, Honest Ulsterman, Envoi, Poly, Poetry File, Phras94, Stand, Ambit, The North, The SHOp, The Interpreter's House, Mslexia, The Poetry Business (with review of collection *Paper Whites*), Blinking Eye, Biscuit Publishing, Poetry on the Lake, HU, Seam (with review of *Because We have Reached That Place*)

Recent Prizes:
Bridport 2011
Stafford International 2011
Torriano 2011
Grace Dieu 2011
Live Canon 2001 and 2011
Bedford open 2011

Contents

Flaming Stargazer	1
Fairy Godmother	2
Rabbits	3
Humpback	4
Smaller Deaths	5
Neglect	6
War Birds	7
The One Fatality	8
Experiment on a Cat	9
A Moment of Tenderness	10
Mahjong	11
Ophelia	12
Black and White	13
Cuddling an Orangutan	14
Snowflake Falling into Fire	15
www.teensyweensy.com	16
Raining Cats and Dogs	17
Instead of Red Roses	18
Feelings	19
Following the Dodo	20
Too many Cats	21
This Much I Know	22
Hedge-Cutting	24
Rough Sex	25
Audubon said	26
A Murder of Crows	27
Gone	28
Now This	29
Uncreated	30
Resurrection	31
The Sick Swan	32
Telling of Ice	33
Watching with the Cat	34
Self Harm	35
Valetta Butterfly	36
Endangered	37
Mozart	38
Nightwalking	39

Always Sea	40
Blind	42
Mole	43
Who am I?	44
Burying My Head in the Sand	47
A Fox Comes To Gaze At Us	48
At the Allied War Cemetery, Soudha Bay, Crete, April 2000	49
Black Birds Dying	50
Telling the Bees	51

Flaming Stargazer
i.m. Nathan Kelley 22.04.61 – 14.12.85

This Christmas he's been dead
longer than he was alive.
He had twenty-four years
of learning about fish

and what makes them tick.
Of winters floating in warm seas
where fish were as if
a child had painted them.

In photos he's grinning,
not showing the shark-bite
scars of heroic surgery,
nor the years gasping for breath

drowning in air.
Not showing the weeks treading
water in wards of old men
whose hearts also failed

and where he could not bear
to waste precious time,
but instead read books on fish disease
and the geology of planets.

He shelters now in the shallows of my heart,
and on the oddest of occasions,
for example, when I see a tank of guppies
in a waiting room, a jar of winter daffodils,

or a full moon blueing the bay,
he rises to the surface,
and like his fond goldfish,
Carassius auratus,

the flaming stargazers, whose
celestial eyes followed his every move,
he's still there in the current of life,
with me wherever I go.

Fairy Godmother

Forgive me if I do not bestow
the usual gifts of riches and beauty.

I would rather grant stillness in your life
for regarding small things:

the angle of a wren's tail, for example,
or the slow flowering of lichen,

a quietness in your heart
allowing you to notice snowdrops

lighting the darkness under an apple tree,
how at 4pm on the last day of January

wet sand is the blue of a robin's egg,
how a single bluebell has no smell

but a bluebell wood has a cold fragrance,
how an olive leaf is like a silver fish,

and a severed cypress bract
is the green foot of a hummingbird.

May you be watched over
by the god of simplicity –

a piece of smooth beach glass,
an ermine moth on muslin,

a god who brings joy at the sight of a daisied meadow,
who shows one palm leaf waving while others are still,

and offers calmness
to watch the healing of a snail's broken shell.

Rabbits

Masked by its kill
a stoat jerks on the lane
and for a moment
I think it's a maimed
rabbit and I ought to stop
and put it out of its misery.
The stoat drops
the dead weight
of rabbit to grip
more tightly,
and dragging it,
jinks into a hedge
bright with bluebells
and campion.

It takes me back
to a bleak night
in County Cork,
after midnight, lost,
I'm following
a driver going too fast,
rain sheeting the headlights
of speeding trucks,
sheep like sudden rocks,
and terror in the eyes
of a rabbit with mangled back legs
jerking on the pot-holed track.

Humpback

For days it drifts
and wallows in the bay
nuzzling a buoy.
When it dies
they tow it to the beach.
It measures twenty feet,
the bloated tongue lolling
from the gaping beak,
blowholes blocked with sand,
sloughed skin shredded
like burst rubber tyres,
the long flipper piebald
like the body
and the vulnerable penis.
Blood puddles the sand.
A small dog sniffs
and pisses against its bulk,
white sea-lice infest the furrows
of the ventricle pleats.
A man says you'd catch all sorts
if you touched it.
That night I don't sleep,
listen for the mother blaring.
At low tide chainsaws
and the beam of headlamps.
Nothing left at first light
but caterpillar tracks
and an umber stain
on the white sand.

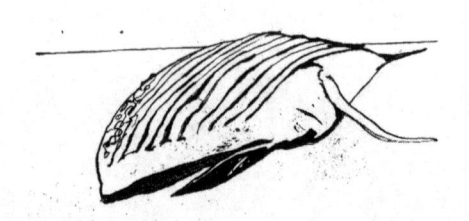

Smaller Deaths

There are other smaller deaths –
the beach littered with empty shells
of Maja squinado, spider crab,
some whole, spiked carapace up,
others with skinny legs relaxed,
waiting like red dogs
to have their bellies scratched,
and more scattered body parts than
you'd hope to see in any slasher movie.

Neglect

The old cat yowls
in the small hours and Dolly,
curled up by my feet, ignores
the call, knowing

her mother is not bringing
a half-dead mouse.
I rouse myself to thank Flo
for the toy because

I never showed enough
love for my children.
I didn't say I love you,
not in so many words,

only cooking good food,
making sure your shoes
fit, and getting you
to school on time.

I love you. Love you.
I never said I love you.
But I didn't bad-mouth
your father to you

and we always ate together.
OK I didn't let you watch
Hawaii 5-0 and had rows
with newsagents who showed

girlie mags at child height,
and probably embarrassed
you in many other ways.
And I never said I love you.

Instead, because it's too late
to start, hoping to make up
for earlier neglect
I make a fuss of this little old cat.

War Birds

In WW1 Germans freed flocks of carrier pigeons from their advancing tanks with details of the Allies' position. The Allies employed falconers in the hope that their birds would intercept enemy intelligence.

It's called stooping:

the hunched swoop
of a peregrine,
the deadly missile.
And after the slaughter,
(feathers scattered
like rose petals)
the executioner
is hooded in leather,
veiled, cowled
like a budgerigar
or caged parrot,
covered for the sake
of peace,
careless talk stopped.

The One Fatality

Macrocarpa – Monterey cypress.
Growth rings showed the tree to be 65 years old.
It had a girth of nearly four metres and an approximate
height of 30 metres. The lightning split the tree from top to
bottom on November 3, 2002

Afterwards, they found the one fatality :
a wood pigeon, which appeared
to be only sleeping, and which Nigel,
the tree-surgeon, roasted with streaky bacon,
parsnips, greens and a salsa of aubergine
peppers and onion. Its meaty breast
had the subtle taste of saltpetre and brimstone.

Experiment on a Cat

Every morning I expect the black
and white cat to fall in the filling bath.
She flirts with fate, balancing
on the slippery edge and reaching down
to take a lick of steaming water.
Her broad bum faces me
and it would be the easiest thing
to give her a little shove,
just enough so she'd lose balance and slide in.
I'm interested to know what she'd do,
after the initial shock.
Would she rise from the deep like the shark in Jaws?
Or would she perhaps discover that fear
of water is an inherited whim? She might
suddenly realise that weightlessness
is rather pleasant, and pussy-paddle around,
her thick coat plastered to her spine,
the black swim-cap of her head,
the seal's whiskers, her sea-green eyes
gazing up at me as if to say,
Come on in, it's lovely.

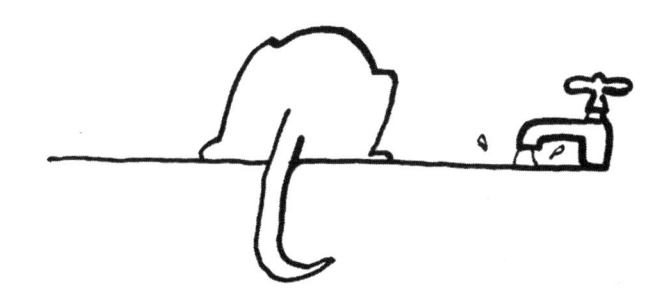

A Moment of Tenderness

Dolly sits on my lap.
She never knew this boy
whose photo I cry over.

It's a favourite one of my children
when they were very young,
recording a moment of tenderness.

But this is about Dolly, my cat,
who knows we are going away.
Unhappiness oozes

from her olivine eyes,
accusing me of betrayal.
I am guilty.

Hers is a simple sadness.
I am here now, soon I will not be.
I, at least, have a photo.

Mahjong

The wooden cottage is on high ground surrounded
by blasted Scots pines whose sawn limbs bleed.
I'm lost in ploughed fields and raise pheasants

and rooks. There's a shed, silvered like an old mirror
and at the window, the surprised eye of an antlered deer.
Other heads lie heaped. It's night. We drink.

A motorboat coughs in Rushy Bay. We have eaten
The sweet meat of local crab. The clink of bone
Mahjong bricks is *the twittering of sparrows*.

Ophelia

I hear a small thud
as it hits the glass
and not finding it
stunned on the deck
think it unharmed
and flown off.

I find the young blue-tit
two days later
in a galvanised
bath of fuschia flowers
and rain water,
a feathered Ophelia.

Black and White

Like piano keys,
a swallow stiff on the step
waiting for me to take it
inside to thaw,
but I'd been away too long,
snow thick under its frozen claws.

Cuddling an Orangutan

Unlikely though it may seem
I was cuddling a baby orangutan
and I woke in a panic sure I had squashed
the hairy infant in my sleep.

My late mother-in-law (the first) who
in this life travelled the world
with her belongings in carrier bags
was with me in the early hours

and my dead son, but he's
always here at night,
and as usual I was trying
to cater for too many guests

with too little food.
One blessing – I wasn't totally
lost, as I am usually through
the long hours of darkness.

Snowflake Falling into Fire

Snowflake
died of skin cancer
in Barcelona Zoo.
The ill-tempered
white gorilla loved yoghurt.
Father of twenty two,
only five survived,
none of them albino.

www.teensyweensy.com

A tiny spider has made a home
in my laptop, entering

the cave of a USB port.
It's dark in there but warm

and I imagine a paradise
of gigabites and digital stalactites

where he'll build a website to trap
dust mites and the occasional virus.

When I log off and shut down
I'll press ctrl/escape

as I can't bear to think of him
crawling confusedly

among the trash and spam
lost forever in cyberspace.

Raining Cats and Dogs

It rains for days until drains
are blocked with birman and poodles
and we paddle in pekinese pups.

Gutters overflow with goldendoodles;
roofs sag under the weight of wet water spaniels
sodden shih tzu and sopping schnauzer.

At every window the pitter-patter
of whippets and pomeranians,
a spatter of singapura and sphinx.

Trees tumble under a torrent of tabbies,
siamese and terriers, chow chow,
chihuahuas, miserable manx.

We drown in daily downpours of ginger toms,
dalmations and doberman
dachshunds and dank great danes.

Umbrellas are bowed and broken
by borzoi and beagle, the steady precipitation
of persians who frown even more bad-temperedly than usual,

the splash, drip, drizzle of lhasa apsos.

Instead of Red Roses

In a glass jar
Twigs of ripe chilli-peppers,
Like the speared hearts
Of small birds –
Mistle-thrush, robin, wren.

Listen.
Can you hear them singing?

Feelings

He died
In the snow
In the bike shed

Ginger
Like all the cats
In the road.

He hunted
In the blue field
Beyond the tracks:

Tiddles –
Saved from a long ago
Sea by my sailor dad.

It seems
My father once
Had feelings.

Following the Dodo

The greak auk
The Alaotra grebe
The Ascension flightless crake
The bishop's o'o
The black-fronted parakeet
The Aukland Islands merganser
The colossal moa
The Bonin grosbeak, and
The black mamo, whose yellow feathers
number 450,000 in a cloak from Hawaii
in the British Museum of Natural History.

Too many Cats
After reading George Szirtes on anecdotes of Miroslav Holub

Do you know the best way
of getting rid of a kitten? He says.

No, we answer.

You take them when they are new born
and snip their heads off with a pair of scissors.
 So.

The ensuing consternation,
not to say horror,
is quickly suppressed
because he is a loved man,
and you can forgive a loved one
almost anything.
After all, he may be right

This Much I Know
with thanks to Dennis Sutton, pest control expert

To catch mice, use chocolate,
peanut butter or bread and jam.
They can't get enough of it.

As a last resort,
if the poisons aren't working
use sticky pads to catch their feet

then one crack with a big rubber mallet –
and lights out – more humane
than back-break traps.

The biggest rats are a foot long.
In my experience they don't attack –
rats run.

A dead pigeon can glide for hundreds of metres.
Shoot a problem bird in the head with a shotgun.
That's humane.

I'm against foxhunting,
it's not humane.
I don't believe in reincarnation.

Your first dead human is the worst.
You get hardened after that.
Apart from the flies, pupae, maggots

and body fluid,
the smell
is something you never forget.

If we stopped pest control
in London in a year or two
we'd be overrun.

When a German cockroach mates,
the female lays an egg-case
with thirty young. A rat

couple can have an extended family
of 15,000 within a year.
You'll always need people like me.

Hedge-Cutting

Nevermore blackbird and robin
Nevermore the bullfinch
Or spotted flycatcher

Nevermore the rare invertebrates,
Lesnes's earwig and the Chobham comb-foot spider.
Nevermore the dormouse.

Nevermore peacock, gatekeeper
And brown hairstreak
Feeding on hedgerow nectar.

Rough Sex

The banana slug will bite off its own
penis and leave it in the female
to prevent any other slug depositing DNA.

The humble barnacle has a penis
thirty times its own length.

The male water beetle doesn't take no for an answer.
He has suckers on his feet to allow him to get a grip
on the female's carapace.

In response, she has developed ridges on her back
so she can dislodge him if she finds him unappealing.

Male snakes have a forked penis
as well as a forked tongue, possibly using both
to prevent the female from escaping.

Audubon said

A single flock
of passenger pigeons

numbered over a billion.
The sky black with them

for three days.
The last one, named Martha

by her keeper, died
in 1914 at Cincinnati Zoo.

A Murder of Crows

I'm on the deck looking
at the kerfuffle
on the beach:

an injured gull and three
strutting crows out
to finish it off.

The gull, anchored
to sand by a broken wing,
raises a desperate beak.

The crows back off
then back they come
to lunge at its eyes

while above
herring gulls and terns
hugger-mugger

plunge and screech.
The crows swagger
and the sand is pink.

The gulls flock
to glut on a purple
slick of fish.

Gone

The Tasmanian tiger wolf.
The Caribbean monk seal.
The hairy-eared dwarf lemur,
eaten by Madagascans
and losing its habitat
to deforestation.
and soon the golden-rumped
elephant shrew.

Now This

It's early summer and town roofs are full
of black-back and herring gull.

We don't get them out here
except for the loner that comes each day

but this time of year young learn from old.
Over us, hundreds gather at dawn

and you hear the breaking voices as they learn
to haunt peregrine and sky-surf

or they rest on wet sand, a couple of adults
among them, learning other stuff:

how to speak in tongues. You can hear the elders chant,
warn, laugh, the low moan of one talking to himself.

Now this: it's midday, mid-tide, more or less,
a raft of young birds, herring gulls mostly,

form a funeral cortege, a dark bruise on velvet.
The corpse lies, breast up, drowned.

Now other gulls come, pall-bearers
guiding for a long hour, maybe their first dead

on a last high flight on the falling tide.
The only adult, perhaps its mate,

floats close, white breast nudging the young aside.

Uncreated
Due to Warming, El Nino Southern Oscillation and the Chytrid fungus, the barely two inch toad of Monte Verde rain forest was last seen on May 15 1989.

Martha Crump, ecologist
And herpatologist

Saw one hundred and thirty-three
Golden toads of Costa Rica.

Neon bright and shiny
As if dipped in Day-Glo enamel,

Mating in a kitchen-sink sized pool
Which dried up five days later

Leaving behind the eggs,
Desiccated and covered in mould.

Conservation status:

Uncreated. Extinct.

Resurrection

Setting insect traps
at the Navy's Defence
Fuel Supply Point

last Easter,
a visiting professor
spotted the blue-winged,

black-dotted butterflies.
Sun broke through
and there they were,

a small cluster
cavorting among the milk vetch
in tall grass at San Pedro,

the Palos Verdes blue butterfly,
eleven years after
being declared extinct.

The Sick Swan

I carry it
wrapped in sacking.

It has lost weight and needs me.
I carry it all

the long night.
The swan is as light

as its feathers
but I am exhausted.

Telling of Ice

Was it you said that gulls gather
over the house of someone about to die?

Now they're here at dusk,
loudly complaining about the coming dark,

hundreds of them, like pterodactyls,
pterodactyls

telling of ice and dark.
A bleak cloud comes to swallow

the birds, once white, now black
and here comes the dark.

Watching with the Cat

Cat agrees, there is something inherently calming
 about test cricket on the telly.
We are lulled by the rhythm of a bowler running,
the release of ball, its flight, the sudden thrust of bat,
the satisfying clunk as ball hits middle and flies.
Perhaps the red ball is for my cat a parrot

or a plump robin, that one man threw, another hit
and yet another caught. Perhaps he thinks these white-
furred men are almost cat when they play the sport.
For five days we lounge and slump, he on my chest
stopping me from ever getting up
and ironing or cooking supper,

and we share the slow battle
of the drama, the drone of the presenter.
Cat leaps as I groan or cheer at every wicket lost,
a mighty six on the stadium roof, a diving catch,
and sulks for a while under the sofa
until I settle again into an almost slumber

when he returns to march, claws drawn, on my lap.
You can tell by his narrowed eyes he thinks
the ball has had more than enough of flight and freedom
and knows the white cats will toy with it until it dies.
We snooze together and watch, one eye closed
the remains of the day's play, bails removed, purrs, applause.

Self Harm

A caged parakeet
not allowed to fly.
He makes a mess.
Who's a naughty boy?
Plucking his breast feathers.
Think of a child kept in a chicken hut
a child with his wings clipped
a child with no laugh
his hurt heart.

Who's a pretty boy?

Valetta Butterfly

I do not come across
the endemic swallowtail,
though a cabbage white
with black veins
alights on my hand,
tastes the inside
of my wrist,
the blue veins.

Endangered

*Elephants
Pliny says
know the
difference
between
right &*

*wrong & they
worship the
stars & pray to the sun
& the moon*

        WG Sebald

Where once was the shade of umbrella thorn,
the scent of rain, a waterhole
where they rolled in mud,
and yellow butterflies on heaps of dung,

now is a tobacco tin shaped like a capstan,
a ship's wheel clock that no longer ticks,
moon is the wrong shape, flickers or is dead,
stars are gone and a cold sun hangs overhead.

In single file
a broken tusked bull,
a matriarch who's lost an eye,
a calf missing a mother of pearl toe

no longer trumpeting and long forgotten
they tiptoe on mantelshelves
in Maidenhead and Godalming

Mozart

Picnic in the rain,
Mozart in the park.
Broken umbrellas
fruit bats hang
above us on
eucalypts in the dark.

Nightwalking

Piles of elephant dung
steamed in headlights
as I drove through
silent London streets.
I thought of Africa,
the golden butterflies
swarming over warm
droppings, and pansy
butterflies, yellow
and purple, a handful
of flung confetti,
and the dung-beetles
juggling their loot,
and I drove around
the huge, unlikely
heaps and came upon,
like in a dream,
a procession of
elephants tip-toeing
along a sleeping street.
Whose bed I had come
from I forget,
but not elephants
nightwalking in London.

Always Sea

Standing high
at the end of
each narrow lane
is Sea, barely keeping
itself to itself

and often falling
into funerals,
weddings,
clotted cream tea.

Sea throws dolphins
into the air
with boats,
fathers, sons, prayer.

A sudden squall
and harbour ghosts
run under water
from Westcott's Quay
to Smeaton's Pier.

Black, tabby, tortoiseshell,
Cat is King
of lane, steep steps
and windowsill.

But even Cat
bows down to Gull.
Gull owns granite cliff,
sky and all the lichened roofs.

Gull is loud
Lord of Love Lane,
Mount Zion, Saint Eia,
Salubrious Place, and Bellair,

Barnoon, Barnawoon,
Wheal Dream, Virgin Street,
The Island and Ayr,
and the white sands of Porthminster,

Porthgwidden, Carbis
and Porthmeor.
All the lovely names
still there, still there.

And always Sea at the end...
always Sea standing
high at the end
of each cobbled lane...

Sea, Sand, Sky

Blind

I wish I had held you
a little longer
in my hands.
You were smaller
than I imagined
with your pink
mitten paws,
the sharp claws
I was wary of,
the shoving snout.
I don't know how
you came to be
by the back door.
You cringed
as I picked you up,
shy, plush creature.
I imagine you now
pushing at the bluebell
bulby soil,
bulldozing
your way through
silty sod, doing
what we all do,
living on, blindly.

Mole

It would take at least
a hundred of you
to make a small
pair of trousers.
I would rather
think of you
shaping
mossy nests
for your plushy young,
paralysing worms
with your toxic
saliva
and storing them
by the thousand
in deep larders.
I hear that you
squeeze the worms
between your navvy paws
to rid them of soil.

I hear that a worm will leap
into the air to escape your grip.
I'd love to see that.

Who am I?
'Matter never dies, it just changes form.' Einstein

I am almost nothing,
Bacterium, Germ.

I am eaten by Fly.
Now I am Fly.

Swallowed by Swallow.
Now I am Swallow flying

south to warm skies.
I am flying high, high,

killed and eaten
by a stalking Hawk.

Soaring higher and higher
now I am Peregrine, raptor

nesting on a cliff edge
raising a family,

then shot,
shot by a farmer.

I lie on the beach and rot
and for a while I am Not.

I am Not
I am Not.

But I am Bacterium, powerful
and poisoning.

I am washed out by waves.
Now I am Sea

rising and falling,
fierce and gentle,

mighty and destroying,
I am Sea.

Sea, Sea, Sea
I am Sea.

I am eaten by a mackerel,
A shining silver mackerel.

I am Fish, swift and powerful,
I am Mackerel.

I am eaten by Tuna
I am big fish, I am Tuna.
I am hooked by a fisherman,
a hungry, hungry fisherman,

I am lying in the bilges,
dying, dying.

I am eaten by the fisherman's child.
I am Child, Child

laughing and playing,
laughing and playing.

I am Bacterium,
Fly and Swallow,

Peregrine Hawk and Ocean,
Fish and Fisherman's Child.

And when Child grows to be fisherman
I will be Fisherman,

and when Fisherman dies
I will be almost nothing,

But I will still be Bacterium,
I will still Be,

I will always Be
I will always Be.

Matter Doesn't Die

Cold bright January –
The butterfly found
Behind the mirror yesterday.

Burying My Head in the Sand

It makes you sneeze at first and your eyes
feel gritty as if you haven't slept for days,

but when your brain accepts the revelations
your organs stop panicking and it seems you've been here

forever, burrowing with rag and lug, passing
time with lugubrious sea cucumber, eye to frowning eye with
    crab,

waiting with the weever – barb
primed to strike a carefree paddler.

I partner a young mussel dancing on its byssus,
before it settles with its elders and betters

and thread-like legs chain it to rock
or mother, bivalve brothers and sisters.

The downside is the prevalence of poly-
styrene chip cartons, knotted condoms

and the odd headless Barbie.
But there are compensations:

caresses from a wriggling dab or blenny,
star-like polyps shooting from dead men's

fingers, surf pounding in the shell of your skull.

A Fox Comes To Gaze At Us

on the same path the badger walks at night
when he comes for scraps at the back door;
the fox looks lean and hungry, but they always do.
He noses the air and earth, takes off along the lower path,
stops to look through a gap in the hedge
as if admiring the view,
or maybe he's shocked that the big trees are gone.
We still feel the loss.
He leaps back, knock-kneed, as if he's sick or hurt,
but it's just the old cat, Flo, standing up to him,
side-on, humping her slight back,
plumping her tail big as a fox and hissing till he backs off,
tail between orange legs.
We sit in our light box, whipped by light
bounding on the white walls, trapped like wild birds,
drowning like netted fish,
as light floods the colourless water of the room.

At the Allied War Cemetery, Soudha Bay, Crete, April 2000

On what would have been his birthday
I salute other mothers' sons at Soudha Bay,
some only *'Known unto God'*. A grey
heron posts as sentinel, a hoopoe hoots reveille,
scent of vanilla lifts from spiny broom
and oranges gleam over soldiers lying far from home.

We have seen wild tulips, a red anemone,
a chaffinch led us down a rocky valley
where crown daisies reign and in gloomy
shade a dragon arum's black tongue curves.
Carved on a headstone – *'He leaves*
A white unbroken glory, a gathered radiance.'

We listen to silver olive trees, ache to see
the nightingale that breaks our hearts in a eucalyptus tree.

Black Birds Dying

A leafless tree
Noisy with black birds
In the winter dawn.

Silence sinks like a knife.
One by one they fall.
Dead birds blacken the lawn.

Telling the Bees

I had to tell the cats –
like telling the bees.
They knew, anyway,
but saying the words made it real.

The large tabby lowered his head
and with it comforted my hand.

The old English tradition of 'telling the bees' after a death was supposed to stop the bees abandoning the hive.

Oversteps Books Ltd

Oversteps has previously published books by the following poets: David Grubb, Giles Goodland, Alex Smith, Will Daunt, Patricia Bishop (2), Christopher Cook, Jan Farquarson, Charles Hadfield, Mandy Pannett (2), Doris Hulme, James Cole, Helen Kitson, Bill Headdon, Avril Bruton, Ross Cogan (2), Ann Kelley, Marianne Larsen, Anne Lewis-Smith, Mary Maher, Susan Taylor, Simon Williams, Genista Lewes, Alwyn Marriage, Miriam Darlington, Anne Born, Glen Phillips, A C Clarke (2), Rebecca Gethin, W H Petty, Melanie Penycate, Andrew Nightingale, Caroline Carver, John Stuart, Ann Segrave, Rose Cook, Jenny Hope, Christopher North, Hilary Elfick, Jennie Osborne, Elisabeth Rowe, Anne Stewart, Oz Hardwick, Angela Stoner, Terry Gifford, Michael Swan, Denise Bennett, Maggie Butt, Anthony Watts, Joan McGavin, Robert Stein and Graham High.

Ann Kelley's last poetry collection, *Because we have reached that place*, was published by Oversteps Books in 2006.

For details of all these books, information about Oversteps and up-to-date news, please look at our website:
www.overstepsbooks.com